HAL•LEONARD
INSTRUMENTAL
PLAY-ALONG

VIOLA

STEPHEN SONDHEIM
BROADWAY SOLOS

CONTENTS

THE CD IS PLAYABLE ON ANY CD PLAYER, AND IS ALSO ENHANCED SO MAC AND PC USERS CAN ADJUST
THE RECORDING TO ANY TEMPO WITHOUT CHANGING THE PITCH.

ISBN 978-1-4234-7284-1

RILTING MUSIC, INC.

EXCLUSIVELY DISTRIBUTED BY

HAL•LEONARD®
CORPORATION
7777 W. BLUEMOUND RD. P.O. BOX 13819 MILWAUKEE, WI 53213

Visit Hal Leonard Online at
www.halleonard.com

ANYONE CAN WHISTLE

from ANYONE CAN WHISTLE

Words and Music by
STEPHEN SONDHEIM

VIOLA

BEING ALIVE

from COMPANY

Music and Lyrics by
STEPHEN SONDHEIM

VIOLA

Moderately

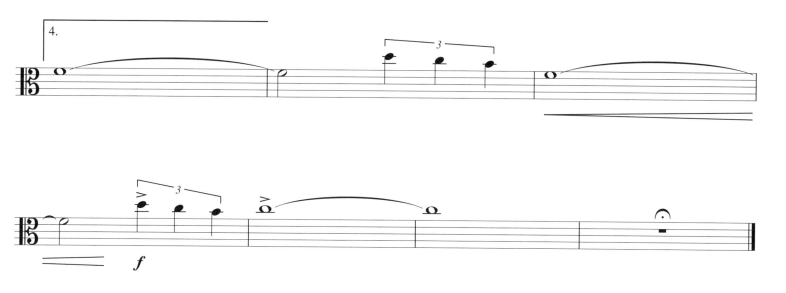

BROADWAY BABY

from FOLLIES

VIOLA

Music and Lyrics by
STEPHEN SONDHEIM

CHILDREN WILL LISTEN
from INTO THE WOODS

VIOLA

Words and Music by
STEPHEN SONDHEIM

COMEDY TONIGHT
from A FUNNY THING HAPPENED ON THE WAY TO THE FORUM

Words and Music by
STEPHEN SONDHEIM

GOOD THING GOING

from MERRILY WE ROLL ALONG

VIOLA

11/12

Words and Music by
STEPHEN SONDHEIM

JOHANNA
from SWEENEY TODD

VIOLA

Words and Music by
STEPHEN SONDHEIM

LOSING MY MIND
from FOLLIES

VIOLA

Music and Lyrics by
STEPHEN SONDHEIM

Slowly, with feeling

NOT A DAY GOES BY

from MERRILY WE ROLL ALONG

VIOLA

Words and Music by
STEPHEN SONDHEIM

NOT WHILE I'M AROUND

from SWEENEY TODD

19/20

VIOLA

Words and Music by
STEPHEN SONDHEIM

OLD FRIENDS
from MERRILY WE ROLL ALONG

VIOLA

Words and Music by
STEPHEN SONDHEIM

PRETTY WOMEN

from SWEENEY TODD

Words and Music by
STEPHEN SONDHEIM

VIOLA

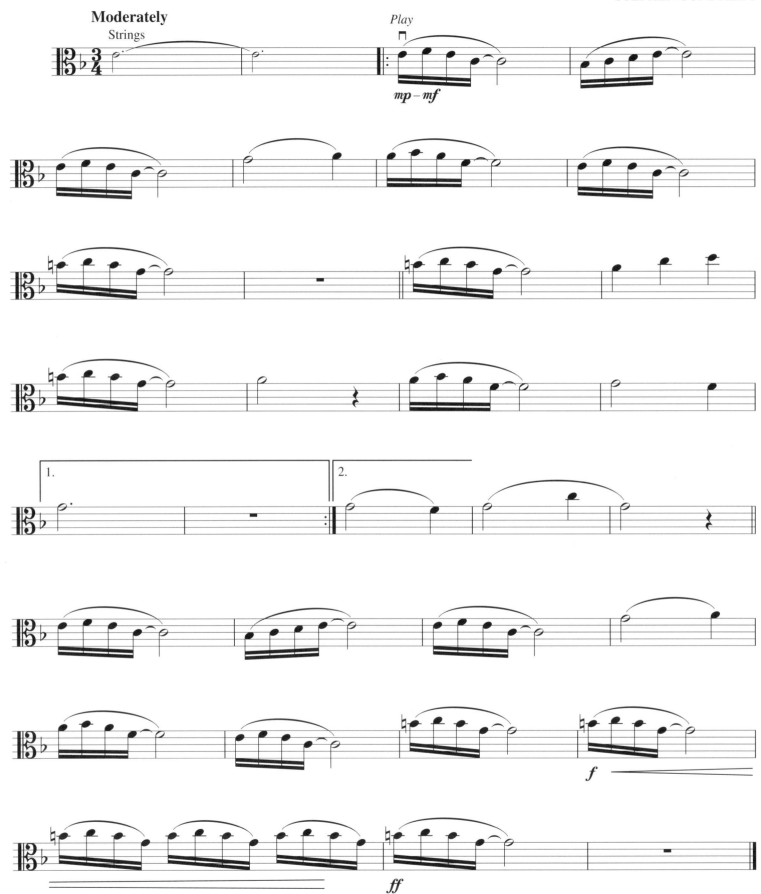

SEND IN THE CLOWNS

from the Musical A LITTLE NIGHT MUSIC

Words and Music by
STEPHEN SONDHEIM

SUNDAY
from SUNDAY IN THE PARK WITH GEORGE

VIOLA

Words and Music by
STEPHEN SONDHEIM

Slowly with feeling

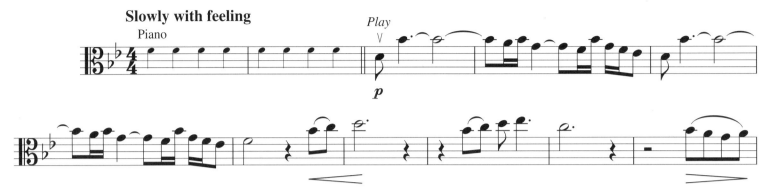